Where, the Mile End

Julie Morrissy

Where, the Mile End

Book*hug Press
2019

FIRST EDITION

Book*hug Press acknowledges the land on which it operates. For thousands of years it has been the traditional land of the Huron-Wendat, the Seneca, and most recently, the Mississaugas of the Credit River. Today, this meeting place is still the home to many Indigenous people from across Turtle Island, and we are grateful to have the opportunity to work on this land.

LIBRARY AND ARCHIVES CANADA CATALOGUING IN PUBLICATION

Title: Where, the mile end / Julie Morrissy.
Names: Morrissy, Julie, author.
Description: First edition. | Poems.
Identifiers: Canadiana (print) 20190057343 | Canadiana (ebook) 20190057351
    | ISBN 9781771664677 (softcover) | ISBN 9781771664684 (HTML)
    | ISBN 9781771664691 (PDF) | ISBN 9781771664707 (Kindle)
CLASSIFICATION: LCC PR6063.O7975 W54 2019 | DDC 821/.92—DC23

PRINTED IN CANADA

for John

i

used

to

move

like

this

through

the

world

This

Like

Move

I

Now

Contents

Steel Skin

wind stirs the sand at Bull Island
sending it scattering like snakes in all directions
winter blooms in Dublin
unfolds into a chilly whisper
prompts me to throw on a scarf, or whatever

it's about time to see the cold
not puffs of breath released to the atmosphere, to the city
but time to see the spread
of deadness

transatlantic air directs feelings per season
October to December = regret, austerity, discipline
it is a time to sit up straighter, to breathe carefully
a time to remember that you cannot forget
because the frozen air remains always
in lungs, lying quietly at the base
a film coating organs

in winter it evaporates into your system
travels to the tips of fingernails
to the corners of eyeballs
to that little triangle of muscle in your ear
it comes with strict instructions
a way of being

the Mississippi freezes over
every year
probably worse now than then

probably harder probably thicker
the Mississippi freezes over *every year*
the air from the ten-minute walk across the Washington Street bridge
from east bank to west bank
from comfort to law
a morning mission in ski jackets through a sheltered tunnel
encased in thin panes of glass

some tiny piece of air must have slipped in
between the wrought-iron bars
it must have crept through the cilia in my throat

down
                 down

into my iron truss lungs

Looped

there is a twist that creeps around me
that drags me back to the north strand
where I have never been before
to a park called St. Anne's
a saint I never saw before
a branch, a tongue
a child I never had before

we rehearse for the loop
the Easter Rising hero who keeps
being decapitated by the locals
the council replaces the bust each time
regifting dignity to this statue
only to find a swastika on his neck a week later
his head dumped at his feet

the touch is real
though the sun tricks me
in my childhood bedroom
everything leads back to Bull Island
and the North Strand

Other Half

I used to swim
and swim and swim
over archways
under tunnels

blue nights and days clawed through my dreams
toes pressed poolside
push through stinging metal-flat-palm door
clip clop of flip flop

undressed in 6am darkness
pull the wool over my eyes
stretch Lycra suit, slide up legs
breasts in place
straps on shoulders

I used to swim
—religious
raised elbows
dashing forearms
plunge and plunge and plunge again

the second clock
the smell

I spent the days alone
minutes in water
eardrums echoing

frozen in time and structure
like my leg as it rose, straight
whip-kicked beryl
wet hair spiking the route home

where I closed the internal door behind me
on Admiral Road
in the hexagon apartment
with two double beds

windows everywhere
snow outside

inside
the murmur of the fridge

Intermural

at first—

those six men
white, wilted, thick skinned
huge chunks of flesh and mind
faded eyes they are so much behind

always the same clothes; old suits or slacks
untucked shirts w/ coffee stains
their unkempt blood vessels burst
hands gesture, accents change
from boom to timbre

I am contained by these men
crawl behind them
arms and nails stretched and digging
burrowing into graves
staring at the blue sky of Dundalk and Derry
waiting for them to peer downward
to knock dirt and soil into my mouth

their bodies weigh on mine
a burden that is with me on the 46A
my modest giddiness
as I try to breathe the same air
to know the same unknown

Mechanical Boats / B-Theory

i

the seal is dead & not dead
it comes   and comes
over and back
daily   dashing
as if on string

us—
we look out   to the lake
the boat or ferry on a track   or line
or something

is that boat on a string?
in waterpulled
is there a track   or a system?

turn back to CNN
Hillary's emails
consider eco-policy of the hotel
hang white card on door

DO NOT DISTURB

ii

~~the same time we leave~~
~~she sends away~~
~~for help~~

at lunch steak salad
roast for dinner
stick w/ fish
hangovers kill
not for her   who drinks
tea   at the moment
the visiting Irishman
thinks   we are wild

iii

in 2019 I will be—
that's alright
K & I don't believe in chronological time
I think, maybe—Foucault!
                    Benjamin!
but it's not
it's like   it's like
she says
things happen
before   they happen

we also think the dog talks
through her breath
with words

how much changes
in three years
anyway?

Waterloo Sunset's Fine

it's Tuesday morning
and every lawn mower, grass cutter
and grasshopper in the neighbourhood
is jamming outside
my window

Moving Day

it is straightforward:

> boots or die
> boots or your toes stick together
> like tongues on ice
> boots or an all-inclusive
> with trays of crab claws and prawn cocktail
> delicious sweltering heat just a plane ride away

I write letters home
inquiring about the hand-held heat packs from childhood
postage costs one dollar eighty-five cents
and five to seven business days—not counting Family Day
another provincial quirk

like the Wine Rack
and the difference between the store and the dép
I meet my friends at Aunties & Uncles and pretend—
pour Aunt Jemima's over my pancakes

> this is not maple syrup
> this is regular syrup

I sit on the steps of my walled-in apartment
in Montréal, they are all corridors
in Toronto, walk-in wardrobes
keep sifting through six people's mail
waiting for the heat pack to arrive

Lucky Number Seven

in the line for Costa Coffee
I turn down the corners of my loyalty card
the hospital swims with masks and stethoscopes
this is coffee number eight
I will get to ten by Friday

the warfarin clinic smells like a home brew
of soap, hairspray and ointment
a Mexican wave of yellow booklets on blood thinners
each old lady emerges smiling
holding the crook of her grey arm

the change machine makes promises
a tower of metal from the eighties
something you'd expect to find in the corner of an arcade
in Laytown-Bettystown
beside the one-armed bandit and
the floors of those bumper cars
sprinkled with sand

False Positive

it is one of those evenings
in a slightly-too-hot function room
on the first floor of a Georgian building
overlooking a Dublin park

everyone here is a high achiever
not business-card high achievers
but definitely
a bunch of big brains

one esteemed colleague introduces another
and I wonder how I can slip my name
onto that chain letter

I make sure not to lean on one knee
even out my hips
nod
at the references
I know I've seen the Photo League somewhere—

> everyone in this room
> is bigger
> than me

the not-quite-beige, not-quite-mustard carpet
boasts indentations from years of use
dozens, no hundreds, of applause-filled evenings
incisive Q&As

little grooves where chairs pressed in
and one outstanding red wine stain
sprawling in front of my feet
almost black
a CT scan with shadows

and the heat in the room peaks—

Ca(non)

it's time for us to stop
meeting new people
who perpetuate blandness while we sit
      on fault lines

to count heads before taking on
Shakespearean sonnets and other tropes of arrogance
      groaning vague instructions

breathe;

before nursing old motors back to cheap health
so we can screw on our fingers and toes
and take them some place

      nuclear waste may be our greatest source of temptation
      it longs to be disturbed
      and trickle into our nests

      at Chernobyl, albino storks swing
      while wolves and wild boar vibrate
      through the red dust forest

I urge my friends to take note
over cinq á sept   on Fridays

Joint

we suck the sliver of air from the skylight
the tiny bar of life that slips through
shake in our sleep
fingers wrapped, legs folded
hands sticky with chicken grease
and weed—

    even the law can't hold us now
    not the bright 1 AM sky, not the dynamo
    on the phantom bike that disappears into bushes
    not the swans on the lake, not the road
    not the walk home
    or the clock

    the guy in Luigi's gives us a deal
    we crouch in the alleyway
    holding the joints in our birdlike grip;
    in the emerald night, a swan shutters and snaps
    his yellow beak blinks in the distance

The Anonymist Manifesto

we write from the site of the crash
oxygen masks abandoned at the last second
high from the gas
we laughed maniacally

                as we nosedived
                into the forest

    we sit here, snow as the insulator
    playing out the rest of our lives

    we identify as vegan but hunt all day and night
    rabbits and deer
    skinned and cooked on a self-started fire

    there is a clearing in the woods
    —a cold, open white space
    we set up cities at every corner, behind every tree

    I wake up under the bridge over the Mississippi
    take a short walk to Dinkytown
    turn my head when branches crack
    and I am at the baseball diamond in Prospect Park
    slamming balls over the fence onto the highway

    on what we think are Sundays
    we tumble through the Bowery
    drinking from litre bottles of wine
    in doorways of West Queen West

we are not leaving
the forest is our present and we dance in the trees

Bang! Bang! The Machine!

Landed

open palms gesture for chocolate and pencils
staring at pearly whites
big black eyes flutter and blink
twisting through paddy fields
in white vans with sullen windows
holding everything in
air tight
and sealed from the dirt

it's a tax issue now
some pages blank and several stamped
separate plastic cards for going in and out
yo-yoing between personalities

               which one this time

                              which accent

               which name

swirling into an empty apartment
with IKEA units called Lack
outside, jaundiced streets linked by radios and meters
a maelstrom of taxis like sand dunes
rolling through wide avenues
jig-sawed together
only the colour makes them recognisable

waiting for the chance to pledge allegiance to the flag
with its bursts of colour

dreading the decision between tawny browns and malachite greens
the glazed images of that place
and the assertive reds and whites
assaulting these classrooms

out here, the shade is yellow
with a gloss
behind it
there's teeth

Waterloo Sunset's Fine

walk through shared hallways, clock
the smell of Dettol and bleach
fresh paint
worry about the lease and
how much time
we have left

The Line

my hands move either miles ahead
or miles behind my brain
maybe it began with lead marks on craft paper
at a desk somewhere
in school or at home
before my attention turned
a quick switch and click

my pupils migrate to the sides of my eyes
catching a glimpse of a frill
                            just outside my vision
learning by accessing things
I already know
if I shake my head hard enough
they'll slip out onto the page

like the day I picked up a pencil
and sat, stretching my brain into downward dog
then plow pose then feathered peacock

nowadays
I rifle through drawers at my parents' house
filled with used corks
lemon reamers, spaghetti spoons
throwing open each cupboard door
on a never-ending search for the re-homed sugar

I turn handles
I know approximate locations

somewhere here
in the space between
the oven and the new French doors

Mission

the shiver at the back stairs of City Lights
in a wooden room where career people shrug
at Ferlinghetti's empty chair
after his fall at the post office
tell me I might see him when he gets better

every five minutes I dance around the room
singing at the publisher
Lawrence Ferlinghetti has touched this!

stacks of photos from the sixties
white smocks and wiry beards
I painfully research copyright, draft formal emails
to photographers and families of people
I can't imagine cared much for asking permission

        back on the curb, I wait to return the vacuum cleaner
        the confusion it causes when I call it a Hoover
        as though I am looking for a very specific way
        to suck up the dirt from my carpets

        steam rises from concrete
        obscuring my view of men gathered
        drinking coffee at the end of the block
        I swish by, conscious of my legs bruised

        from nights running the bases at Potrero Hill
        chugging blue Gatorade between home runs

until my right knee buckles and condemns me
to a season of squinting and hand signals
under a swinging bat

at the corner of Broadway and Columbus
at the corner of Potrero and 25th
at the corner of Shotwell and Precita
at the corner of Mission and Cesar Chavez

Lippincott

behind the house on Bathurst
you can walk in a square
come back by the Ulster Coin Wash

in October of that year
I walked that square-alley-block
to escape the panic in my room
when I thought I was sick
when I visited the doctor twice a month
convinced the first one
was wrong
one more to check my blood
I took a lot of numbers

      in the evenings
      the route home from Robarts
      I bought buns with chocolate icing
                pink sprinkles

the snow melted
revealing a different square
Bickford Park
up and down newly green slopes
to the beat of a voice on an running app

      Walk 2 minutes

        Run

Walk   30 seconds

Run

Cooler, 80 Days

in 1994 I watched celluloid men dig in darkness
rehearsing confrontations with soldiers
tricks to stay covert
       German first, never English
I learned to be brave from *The Great Escape*
and to fake it

like the men huddled under the surface
tunnels collapsed as they wheeled to freedom
and when disaster struck—
they came up short
       the tunnel didn't reach
the Nazis found the loose tile

I hovered in our sitting room on tiptoes
square-eyed, willing them to stop
just wait in the camp, the war ends
tapping at the curved glass
              just wait

in the end, only three got away
the rest—stopped at train stations, fields, borders
forgetting the lessons they had learned
the hours spent practising

their fate sealed
in one fast moment
when instinct set in

A Retrospective

I think of you as gesture
a certain contortion of your face
the downward slant in your eye
I think   of you

in a way that should not even be a "you"
it should be "him"

I think, in this small city it is inevitable
that I will run into you
our paths will cross   in an unexpected moment
likely with some form of audience
maybe with partners or old friends or new ones

if I were to run into you alone
it would be different
I would embrace with abandon
without thought of how it looks to others
or how it looks   to you

I think of you not because of   love
or longing
it is deeper than that   cloistered
it is because when I open my palm here
and hold my hand out
the air settles
                         deep

          into the ruck

Flat One, Six am

do those moments belong
to some place else   some body else
a giggle I don't recognise
a dance I've never seen
skin against a door
a split-second stirred

half thoughts
      half words
            half smiles

      hang in air I can't touch
            air within—

cool blue surrounds a kitchen counter
at unexpected corners, my eyes cry
the sting of smooth leather

that counter
      that counter

      asserts itself, resolute
      a boat in a basement
      the roll and pitch of bodies

some days
I turn the corner
at Bathurst and Ulster, fall flat on my knees
palms smack sidewalk

pop

Laundry-Garbage-Brew

aaaaaaaaaaaa   but it shifts

    doesn't it?

the turning point
the intersection, what corner
how many times I biked down Manchester Avenue
on the way to Dupont   uphill
coasting home, half drunk half exhausted
peddles churn. Churn. CHurn.
making my brain smarter
should have waited on the bridge or at that bus stop
got married in Wisconsin in 2004 for the free keg of beer

crackkkkkkkk   (that's a hard 'k')

like ice but not a barrier
another   formed   thing   framed
in underground car parks, emails, Skype calls
next to the snow boots I resisted buying
the wool socks
REAL socks
(because the previous pair purchased were not considered real)
what fresh basement is this?
right now it's the one where my damp underwear is locked
in a plastic drum
captive
furiously turning knobs
that sound like the wheel of fortune at the annual xmas fair

in the hall of Saint Mary's Primary School
with those square wooden numbers
reusable   low cost luck

        if I could put my fist through this plastic bowl

Wake

nobody is from where I'm from
the density of the cold, the snow murmurs
secrets under my feet
directions to nowhere

chicken coop brains flap their wings
bits of fluff and feathers float
you can swallow them, lick around them
but it won't feed you

I will send letters out, see what comes back
which ones I can add to my brain
I want a longer line that stretches
past the death of a field, to the other shore

there are warnings for bears, snakes, cockroaches, bed bugs
but where is the water—
it lies there, dead in snow
the rats in the canal know more about it
than we do

taps turn on Bathurst
clouds emerge, fill my glass
with fluoride and snow;
blink and smile

at the story of the academy
          meanwhile, my mind is flown
by the men in sensible, brown shoes
gathered at the soft mud of Mossbawn

Art Hole

once jammed with bicycles
a dilapidated garage nestled beside the oil tank
beaten by the cold
Greek goddesses reminding us you cannot learn in heat
wind roared through windows
as we maintained order on the shelves
kept paint in the dark
stockpiled books on Basquiat, Bevilacqua, Bresson

we learned to live off the land
our agrarian beginnings born inside those peppered walls
       flat
like dolmens angled together
mirrors to look backwards
brushes washed and dried with urgency
pockmarks of acrylic congealed
in haphazard swatches on a cement floor

wary of straight lines
we crosshatched details
ignored the vexing smell of turpentine
and when the gas ran out
we painted fires

Waterloo Sunset's Fine

wake to chirps of squeaky wheels
on supermarket floors
a new family moves in
outside our window
nesting in tropical-forest-wonder

Stockholm

there's a hand on the back of my neck
but it won't hold me down
it guides me through the new neighbourhood
the back roads and tiny windows
onto deserted Luas tracks
where we walk single file, tripping over gravel
careful not to fall

to break my skin that won't stop bleeding
blood so thin it can't help welling up
       inside me
pouring out into the spaces between the stones
I kneel, try sweep it up with my hands
suck it back into my body
save it for later;
when we are under the skylight

swatting away the feeling
of thumbs sunk in skin
the horseshoe grip

French Braid

red hair, Irish skin
routinely trained into new tan lines
and old freckles

Joan's fingers twist precise plaits
while we swat away Factor 50
avoiding the shadow cast
by the brim of her sun hat

all schooled in catholic systems
myself, Odharnait, Joan
                         by the nuns
the same order
that bottle-blue pinafore, shirt, dickie bow
no boys

a look exchanged when Claire says
her mother was a Tevlin
it doesn't exist in Ireland
—maybe once

as

               O'Teibhlinn   or   Shevlin

she scrunches her sweet Québécoise face
I tell her she'll see when she visits
or when I—

the four of us duck from the Greek man
heckling over his balcony
today he's having a BBQ
                    we should come over

instead we pat slapdash on our keyboards
heads down
writing theses in the sun
sipping vodka-Coke floats
careful not to touch the rolled black felt
of the single-ply roof

          Aylmer   Dublin

          Meath   Nairobi

          we climb out the window on Fridays

Keener

creep   creep before a belonging
be—long
          long

              long time coming
a careful stutter to the gauds of Art
polite smile to strongly assert the word
po....

          I can't say it
not to this canary coloured flop
cannot smile and wissssshhhhh
oh to clap and exclaim
adoringly stroke matching handbags and boots
little gold clasps with neat mechanisms to slip through
        open and close
like these little mechanised mouths
born with loudspeakers and microphones
newsprint marks their hands
grubby fingers smudging each other

        don't get me wrong

        it's my grubby little hands
                too

Intersections

your lips join me on bus journeys
sliding my eyes sideways to a vision of you
I wear your imaginary sweater when I get cold
bike alongside you in my head

remember how I like being away
buy groceries and cook cheap dinners
take trips and smile at strangers
and I forget

about that week
when I tried to eat between stares
when I watched how you acted so at ease
willing myself not to knock over my glass

or drop my fork
I think of standing across the street
seeing your body in the window
waiting outside your door

deciding which was the best way to stand
which side of the door
which direction to face
you watched and watched

until I was gone
and now I am back
in a place where nobody cares
how I butter my toast

I Am Where

on a rooftop in Minneapolis I sit with a book
I find a pane of glass that pushes out onto the flat roof—away
from the one million books that I am supposed to be shelving and dusting
and rubbing with Goo-Gone, my sweat drips onto the pulp
the mouth of the Mississippi waves to me as Old Man Ed marvels at
the progression of my neon skin to even oak

      the books move continent and breed with alarming pace
      I buy the bigger version of the Billy bookcase
      accidentally screw the same shelf in backwards
      paint over the exposed chipboard with white acrylic

I am on the roof when the bridge falls into the river
the concrete buckles in stages
bits of road slip towards the two-mile-wide water,
as men and women in suits
screech and jump from their cars, running uphill to the riverbank
an exercise they had been training for on the treadmills at Goodlife
I spring to my feet, knocking my book off the edge of the roof
switch my gaping eyes between book and bridge
transformed into a valley

                glass doors draw back to reveal the dream
between their open and shut I watch the air I had waited to re-breathe
        the snow I had waited to re-see, the cold I had waited to re-feel
the weather had stood still all this time, had continued without me as if
                            I was never there

Removal

the city has given me the silent treatment
for one hundred and eighty-two days
because I refuse to give it the attention it deserves

one hundred and eighty-two days of protection
from the harshness of its words in a language
I certainly speak but cannot understand

the wind carries words so fast
whipping meanings away from me
when all I am doing is trying

to park my rental car overnight
make sense of the instructions on the sign
the horror on the minus thirty-five morning

when the car is gone   vanished
dumped two blocks away
in Little Portugal

I'm handed a ticket
by the end of April the city softens
knows it has been cruel, realizes

maybe we can make it
because the swings in Parc Jeanne-Mance
have been hung up again

and the Bixis are slotted back into position
I still test each step of the spiral walk-up
holding on to the railing for dear life

Waterloo Sunset's Fine

find unexpected support at the hotel bar
where I scrounge free wifi
and the staff intermittently approach

to ask: is everything okay?

a short pause from me
followed by
an affirmation

The Last Resort

I hear the edges of Doonbeg are collapsing
slipping from the links
straight into the Atlantic
you can book a tee time
become a member
it's a sight to behold
a sensory experience

Cooraclare, Brisla, Caherlean

you'll be able to swim to the Aran Islands soon
or walk
on newly formed ocean spit

tiny bits of shale and dust are tumbling
with each swing of a seven iron
each plump pink footstep
and slow roll of ball
Doonbeg is falling
into the ocean

Mullagh, Kilmurray, Shyan

a once in a lifetime opportunity
a mens' and ladies' locker room
for whatever kind of talk
a perfect space to entertain friends
and family

Doolin, Kilkee, Kilbaha

Ophelia says it's coming
you can count the particles
kiss them goodbye
from the relaxed piano room
in casual opulence

some things are just for you

Communion

black is the colour
the night before

I lie awake
concerned I won't remember
the timing of the psalm
do I read the response each time

or does the congregation?
I am not the only one
text messages bounce between us

when to pause, when to bow
it is not tragic
I do not cry

though as we walk in pairs behind the coffin
my breath becomes wooden
overwhelmed by faces—
the men in my family

the four of us
the younger ones

        [my granny would have said young–er
                         silent 'g']

remain in the front pew
our partners behind with the secondary family
we step back

so that the elders can pass after communion
it had not been arranged or checked the night before
all of us know

as the holy line forms up the aisle
the four of us stay

mouths closed

i measc mo dhaoine
after Mairtín O'Direáin

there is another language we can speak
have always spoken
learned at school at the same time
we wrote words on sharp yellow paper
little rectangles for our butter boxes
to take from our ciseáin at going-home time

it is the language of fireplaces sunk in walls
fireplaces that sit on Cork Street
next to new born babies
and mothers having a smoke in Hello Kitty pyjamas
royal blue boxes of Roses past sell-by dates
ward sisters with upside-down watches

stuck in walls of partly demolished buildings
twenty feet up, hearths facing outward
brass and steel grates showing their teeth to passersby
laughing at us
the innards of these buildings
held in so tight, hammered, melted into concrete

they're worth something you know
my mother says as we pass
someone will take those one night
bandits skirting through scaffolding
pulling hunks of metal from fifty-foot walls
to implant   subterranean

in the souls
of new homes

Grounding

he has never lived above ground there
and I have done both
moved up and down and over
away from the damp
from spiders clinging to corners
from the back door the neighbour barged through
from the streets I thought were mine

four walls stand and hold me
the sliding door and the slight glass
the round bar that runs through the middle
firm, steady
I grab to it   use both hands
if something happened within those walls
with the barking dog

and the shuttered windows
with the paint and the words
if something happened
it was the grass and the gate
the front door
it was that I knew—
if I could manage not to slip on the bathroom floor

if I could forget the dent in the window
from the time a pebble hit the centre
the same view framed the same way
but the shine of the glass
makes the detail spin and fizz

the leaves in the driveway press together
curling as inverted parachutes

Celestial

in memory of sad dogs held upside down
angled, stuffed and tucked under gaping armpits
faces bigger than beaks trapped inside gravity
in memory of Baby Doherty
sucking at the golden teat
fish without knowledge
swimming upstream to an old man who stays young
in memory of infants like giants and men like pigs
blown apart on train lines surging forward, to progress
in memory of the clairvoyant dogs of Khao Lak
whispering to each other as they led the way out
in memory of dropped pins, treasure hunts and hoards

it's a pregnant sky
exploding at hinges
where thought and child and word is born
a crackling that sharpens ears and eyes
a book for the beginning

Canada Life

big, bold Canadian flags caress
the minus-twenty air around the local McDonald's
tonguing the red bricks up and down
sorry—*feels* like minus twenty
actual temperature: minus twelve
we need to be told how to feel this kind of cold
roll over these flatlands
cross through plains of snow
lakes of ice
houses in the middle of nowhere
mid-March
close your eyes
close them—
before your eyeballs freeze

       back to the city
back to Coffee Time
back to streetcar lines
back to Canada Life
back to constructed conversations about *fascist corporate bullshit*
back to the red letters of the Grand building
calling from outside the auditorium

G – R – A – N – D

a lifestyle that thrives on The End
sucks and slithers towards it
       the problem is not the endings
but the ones that do not appear on the syllabus

today the auditorium blinds are closed
the Grand building is hidden
        but it's there
behind the window
behind the Canadian air
behind the flat rooftops
behind the central air-boxes

            It is there.

Waterloo Sunset's Fine

when I was a kid
my dad told me
that for one whole year

        Brian Wilson didn't get out of bed

back then
I found that hard to believe

Landscape

there is no turf where I'm from
no sponge fertile ground
my landscape is a tarmacadam road
at the foot of the Dublin Mountains
my childhood home a four-bed semi

I remember the progression
of cars

Montego
       Peugeot
             Renault
                   Prius

and the day my mom arrived
with her very own
ancient Opel Bluebird
the same colour as the Loreto nuns
the same age as me
in my final year of secondary school

I sat up front with her
pleased as punch not be to biking home
past the throngs of teenage boys from the other school
in my brown skirt
and long garbardine coat

when we pulled up to the drive-thru
my heart sang for a cheeseburger
we sat on woolly seats
munching fries in the car park
of a suburban shopping mall

unaware of the blue-grey tint
poised by the mountains
just behind our backs

Kookee

I've been wanting to take a bath

and stew

really lie there and let the thoughts run over me
in the murky water
as my hands crease and my nipples get cold
I've been wanting
not to cleanse but to consider
to get worked up in the hot water
to emerge renewed   and angry

I really beat up on some cookie dough today
battered it with a wooden spoon
I find them hard to hold
the rough unfinished handle
feels like some crusty piece of felt that was left to rot
but today
I wrapped my bony fingers around it
rammed its roundness into
some recipe from a bag
that's so easy

even my husband can do it

MMXIV

it had been washed up onto the shore
against the broken rock face
beyond the seaweed slime and bits of bucket, rope and dirt
the skin on its bottom half peeled back
pecked off, maybe
showcasing the dull pink pallor of this sea beast
half undressed, or half dressed
depending on how it argued its case
the tiny furs that remained covered its wide back, pointy ears
a couple of teeth showing, right eye missing
unclear if it had fallen out before or after death, or had been eaten
or if that was just something that happens
when a seal dies

the wind carried the odour that swirled
around its plump corpse
ready to burst out of what was left of its skin
curdled blood and bloated organs lay threatening underneath
boiling in the midday sun
layers of blubber holding it all inside

but when we stood, and from four feet away
threw a stone onto its belly
the thud was heard from the seashore into the depths of Scrib
and beyond
the Holy Well rippled
sea salt reverberated
the Virgin Mary's hand twitched
a natural urge after the three-decade-long pins and needles

the sound flew up the knitted hills we had skipped over
into the cracks under our feet
through the keyholes in granite
those tiny spaces, still large enough for it to slink through

the stone—medium-sized, light grey, speckled, unremarkable really
remained, flat on the middle of the washed-up body
two pieces of evidence:
victim and interference
interference and victim
half-covered—a real mess

in a few days the stench will pierce the wet air
unbearable, the locals will cover their mouths and noses
tourists will turn back to rental cars

until the nearest flat cap pushes the offending body back
no small effort, mind
he gathers the other men
they stand to contemplate the best course of action
staring at this rotting, full corpse
this gentle hazard
at the edge of the roll of the tide
nodding their wrinkled chins in agreement
heads slightly scratched
eyebrows almost furrowed
Big, big men

The Mile End

that April, we got lost in Québec
quand nous étions encore trois
drove out pretty far on those arrant roads
past barns and turbines and metal tanks
           fields everywhere

we got lost in Québec and we knew we were lost
there was nobody to ask
(even though one of us was Québécoise)

                              backseat driver

           but she didn't know

we were lost in Dublin too
without her
(we are both from this town)

there was something about that car trip

           or am I thinking of Vermont

when we ran into her by chance
in the middle of a snowstorm in Burlington
remember: that basketball team were staying in the hotel
the pool brimming with tall men
and snow all around
digging the car out

turning tires inward   or against

                or

                        I can't remember how to drive
                        in snow

      we roamed around Québec a few more times together
      a little less lost

I should go for heat next time
                but the bugs
and if I'm alone
can't call a neighbour to kill spiders
probably have never even seen some of those insects
maybe I can live in a new build
a sealed off apartment
maybe even one where the windows don't open
a capsule
and all the channels on the TV

and when Superbowl Sunday comes I can have people round
for beer and party mix
and I'll call home
tell them about the ads

recycle the bottles, walk to the store, clean up, read, watch SATC, wash
the dishes (probably only two plates and a roll-up mattress), shop wher-
ever is on the bus route, avoid buying books, find the best phone plan

         breathe in the calescent air and
         think about how grossly welcome I am there

Notes

The "Waterloo Sunset's Fine" poems were inspired by The Kinks song "Waterloo Sunset" and the endless stream of their music, which dominated my childhood.

"Wake" references poems by Harry Clifton and Paula Meehan.

The Luas is the light-rail system in Dublin. *Luas* means "speed."

"The Last Resort" takes language from the Doonbeg Golf Resort website. In October 2017, Storm Ophelia was the strongest east Atlantic hurricane to hit Ireland in 150 years.

i measc mo dhaoine (pronounced: ih mask muh gwee-nah) translates from the Irish language to mean "amongst my people." The poem is a response to Irish-language poet Máirtín Ó'Direáin's "*Faoiseamh a Gheobhadsa*" (fway-shuv yo-va-sa), meaning "To Find Peace." The word *ciseáin* (cish-awn) means "basket." My thanks to Doireann Ní Ghríofa for bringing Ó'Direáin's poem to my attention.

Acknowledgements and Thanks

I am grateful to the editors of the following publications where versions of these poems first appeared: *Abridged, Angle, Canthius, Cyphers, Honest Ulsterman, Poetry Ireland Review, The Dalhousie Review, The Irish Literary Review, The North, The Stinging Fly,* and *White Wall Review.* Some of these poems have also appeared in the pamphlet *I Am Where* (2015). My thanks to Eyewear for publishing that work.

"Celestial" was commissioned by Isadora Epstein and Claire McCluskey as a response to their eponymous exhibition at Talbot Gallery & Studios, Dublin.

"i measc mo dhaoine" appeared in the Irish Book Day 2016 special issue of *The Stinging Fly: In the Wake of the Rising* drawn from *The Stinging Fly,* issue 33, vol. 2, edited by Seán O'Reilly (Solas Nua/ Stinging Fly, 2016).

"I Am Where" and "Steel Skin" were recorded for *The Poetry Programme,* RTÉ Radio.

"Lucky Number Seven" was included in the Fleadh Cheoil na hÉireann Poetry Trail 2018.

My heartfelt thanks to tall-lighthouse and Book*hug, especially to Jay and Hazel for their hard work, openness and kindness.

Thanks to my mentors and teachers: Paul Perry, Dale Smith, Kathleen McCracken, Harry Clifton, Susan Cahill, and to the English departments at Ulster University, University College Dublin, and Ryerson University.

Special thanks to Maureen Kennelly and the team at Poetry Ireland. Huge thanks also to Grace Wilentz for her friendship and help, and to Siobhán Butler, Christodoulos Makris, Ingrid Paulson, and to Colette Bryce.

Thanks to all of the poetry communities in Ireland, Canada, and around the world for their interest in my work, and for hosting me in cities far and wide.

To my very supportive family and friends—in particular, thank you to everyone who has come to my readings, bought books, cooked dinners, given couches to sleep on, celebrated with me, travelled to see me, and stayed up late nights talking about writing and not writing. Each of you are part of this book, and I hope you find yourselves in it.

Lastly, and as ever, thanks to Michael and Virgil.

PHOTO: SIOBHÁN BUTLER

Julie Morrissy is an Irish poet, academic, and critic. She is a recipient of the Next Generation Artist Award from the Arts Council of Ireland. Her debut pamphlet *I Am Where* (Eyewear, 2015) was shortlisted for Best Poetry Pamphlet in the Saboteur Awards 2016. Morrissy holds a PhD in Creative Writing from Ulster University, and degrees in Literature, and Law. She is the Newman Fellow in Creativity at University College Dublin. Her creative and critical work has been published in Ireland, Canada, the U.S., and the UK, and she was selected as a "Rising Generation" poet by *Poetry Ireland Review*. *Where, the Mile End* is her first book. Morrissy lives and works in her hometown of Dublin, Ireland.

Colophon

Manufactured as the first edition of *Where, the Mile End* in the spring of 2019 by Book*hug Press.

Copy edited by Stuart Ross
Cover design by Ingrid Paulson
Typeset by Jay MillAr